Blissful Brownies

This edition published in 2010 for Index Books Ltd
LOVE FOOD is an imprint of Parragon Books Ltd

Parragon
Queen Street House
4 Queen Street Bath
BA1 1HE, UK

ISBN: 978-1-4454-2171-1

Printed in China

Designed by Fiona Roberts
Photography by Bob Wheeler
Home economy by Valerie Barrett and Sandra Baddeley
Additional recipes and text by Christine France

Notes for the Reader
This book uses metric and imperial measurements. Follow the same units
of measurement throughout; do not mix metric and imperial.

All spoon measurements are level: teaspoons are assumed to be 5 ml, and
tablespoons are assumed to be 15 ml.

Unless otherwise stated, milk is assumed to be full fat, eggs and
individual vegetables such as potatoes are medium, and pepper is freshly
ground black pepper.

Recipes using raw or very lightly cooked eggs should be avoided by infants, the elderly,
pregnant women, convalescents and anyone suffering from an illness.

Contents

Baking Basics

Ingredients for Success

Sugars The type of sugar you use depends on what the individual recipe calls for. Use caster sugar where a recipe doesn't specify a particular type, as this is the best for most cakes. Golden caster sugar is useful for adding colour to paler mixtures, and is usually less refined than white caster. Light and dark muscovado sugars are less refined with a soft, fine grained texture and are used to add a richness of flavour and give a golden or deeper brown colour. Soft light or dark brown sugars are refined sugar, coloured and flavoured, and can replace muscovado.

Granulated sugar has larger crystals, so it can leave speckles in some mixtures. If you run out of caster, you can grind granulated in a food processor for a few seconds as a substitute. Demerara is fine for melting methods and to sprinkle for a sweet crunchy topping. Icing sugar is best kept for frostings and sprinkling, as it gives a heavy result in cake mixtures. Finally, honey, golden syrup and maple syrup can replace part of the sugar in some recipes, but may give a heavier result. As they have a sweeter taste, you can use about a quarter less than sugar. They're great for drizzling, too, either on warm brownies straight from the oven or for glazing when cooled, to give a lovely glossy top and rich flavour.

Flours Plain white flour is the usual choice for brownies, but some recipes may state self-raising flour, which has an added raising agent. If you do not have self-raising flour, add 2^1/$_2$ teaspoons of baking powder to 225 g/8 oz of plain flour and sift together to make self-raising.

Fats Most brownie recipes use butter, which is best for flavour, but you can also use a good-quality hard (block) margarine instead. Soft (tub) margarines should only be used where the recipe calls for them, as these need a slightly different method. Low-fat spreads cannot be used in most ordinary recipes, as they have a high water content. Light-flavoured oils, such as sunflower, can be used in some mixtures, particularly those with a melting method, but remember that they have the same fat content as butter.

Eggs Unless your recipe states otherwise, the eggs should be medium sized. For most mixtures, it is best to use eggs at room temperature, as they will hold more air than chilled ones.

Chocolate Not all brownies include chocolate, but the classic ones are chocolate-rich and depend on good chocolate for their flavour and texture. There is a bewildering array of types of chocolate to choose from, so you need to choose carefully.

To put it simply, chocolate is made up of cocoa solids, cocoa butter and sugar, sometimes with the addition of vanilla, vegetable fat and milk solids. Plain or bittersweet chocolate must by law contain a minimum of 34 per cent cocoa solids and as a rough guide, the higher the cocoa solids content, the better the flavour.

So, check out the label before you buy – for the recipes in this book, we recommend using chocolate with at least 60 per cent cocoa solids, and ardent chocoholics will prefer to go for one with at least 70 per cent cocoa solids for that intense kick of dark chocolate.

Techniques and Tips for Top Brownies

Preheating It is always best to preheat the oven for 10–15 minutes before baking, as you will need a hot oven to achieve a good texture. Adjust the shelves to the position you need before turning on the oven; unless otherwise stated, the brownies should be baked on a middle shelf.

Preparing Tins Depending on the mixture, you will need to either grease, grease and line, or grease and flour the tin, so the brownies turn out easily.

Use a light-flavoured oil or melted butter for greasing and brush over the base and sides of the tin with a pastry brush. Use non-stick (silicone-coated) baking parchment for lining tins, as this peels off easily. For brownies and traybakes, you usually only need to line the base of tins. To do this, place the tin on the paper and use a pencil to draw around the base of the tin. With scissors, cut just inside the outline of the shape drawn so the cut paper will fit inside the tin neatly.

If a recipe says you should grease and flour the tin, simply brush with oil or melted butter as above, then sprinkle a little plain flour into the tin. Shake the tin, tipping the flour to coat the base and sides, then tip out the excess.

Techniques for Success

Melting and creaming methods are the ones used most for brownies and the melting method is the easiest. The fat, sugar and often chocolate are melted together first in a pan or a heatproof bowl set over a saucepan of gently simmering water. Remove from the heat and stir in the eggs and dry ingredients, but don't overmix. Work quickly to get the mixture into the oven straight away, as raising agents will start to react as soon as the ingredients are mixed.

The creaming method involves beating together the fat and sugar with a wooden spoon or hand mixer until soft, pale and creamy. Next, the eggs should be beaten in gradually – if they're added too fast the mixture may curdle – and the flour and other ingredients can then be lightly folded in, preferably with a metal spoon to keep in as much air as possible.

sweet indulgence

the classics

chocolate brownies

makes 15

225 g/8 oz butter, diced, plus extra for greasing

150 g/5$^{1}/_{2}$ oz dark chocolate, chopped

225 g/8 oz self-raising flour

125 g/4$^{1}/_{2}$ oz dark muscovado sugar

4 eggs, beaten

60 g/2$^{1}/_{4}$ oz blanched hazelnuts, chopped

60 g/2$^{1}/_{4}$ oz sultanas

100 g/3$^{1}/_{2}$ oz dark chocolate chips

115 g/4 oz white chocolate, melted, to decorate

Preheat the oven to 180°C/350°F/Gas Mark 4. Grease and line a 28 x 18-cm/11 x 7-inch rectangular baking tin.

Put the butter and dark chocolate into a heatproof bowl set over a saucepan of gently simmering water until melted. Remove from the heat. Sift the flour into a large bowl, add the sugar and mix well. Stir the eggs into the chocolate mixture, then beat into the flour mixture. Add the nuts, sultanas and chocolate chips and mix well. Spoon evenly into the prepared tin and level the surface.

Bake in the oven for 30 minutes, or until firm. To check whether the mixture is cooked through, insert a skewer into the centre – it should come out clean. If not, return the tin to the oven for a few minutes. Remove from the oven and leave to cool for 15 minutes. Turn out onto a wire rack to cool completely. To decorate, drizzle the melted white chocolate in fine lines over the top, then cut into squares. Leave to set before serving.

chocolate fudge brownies

makes 16

85 g/3 oz butter,
plus extra for greasing

200 g/7 oz low-fat soft cheese

1/2 tsp vanilla extract

225 g/8 oz caster sugar

2 eggs

3 tbsp cocoa powder

100 g/3 1/2 oz self-raising flour,
sifted

50 g/1 3/4 oz chopped pecan nuts

fudge frosting

55 g/2 oz butter

1 tbsp milk

75 g/2 3/4 oz icing sugar

2 tbsp cocoa powder

pecan nuts, to decorate (optional)

Preheat the oven to 180°C/350°F/Gas Mark 4. Lightly grease a 20-cm/8-inch square baking tin and line the base.

Beat together the cheese, vanilla extract and 5 teaspoons of caster sugar until smooth, then set aside.

Beat the eggs and remaining caster sugar together until light and fluffy. Place the butter and cocoa powder in a small pan and heat gently, stirring until the butter melts and the mixture combines, then stir it into the egg mixture. Fold in the flour and nuts.

Pour half of the mixture into the tin and smooth the top. Carefully spread the cheese mixture over it, then cover it with the remaining mixture. Bake in the preheated oven for 40–45 minutes. Let cool in the tin.

To make the frosting, melt the butter in the milk in a small pan. Stir in the icing sugar and cocoa powder. Spread the frosting over the brownies and decorate with pecan nuts, if using. Let the frosting set, then cut into squares to serve.

pecan brownies

makes 20

225 g/8 oz unsalted butter,
plus extra for greasing
70 g/2 1/2 oz plain chocolate
125 g/4 1/2 oz plain flour
3/4 tsp bicarbonate of soda
1/4 tsp baking powder
55 g/2 oz pecan nuts
100 g/3 1/2 oz demerara sugar,
plus extra for decorating
1/2 tsp almond extract
1 egg
1 tsp milk

Preheat the oven to 180°C/350°F/Gas Mark 4. Grease and line a 28 x 18-cm/11 x 7-inch rectangular baking tin.

Put the chocolate in a heatproof bowl set over a saucepan of gently simmering water and heat until it is melted. Meanwhile, sift together the flour, bicarbonate of soda and baking powder in a large bowl.

Finely chop the pecan nuts and set aside. In a separate bowl, cream together the butter and sugar, then mix in the almond extract and the egg. Remove the chocolate from the heat and stir into the butter mixture. Add the flour mixture, milk and chopped nuts to the bowl and stir until well combined.

Spoon the mixture into the prepared tin and smooth it. Transfer to the preheated oven and cook for 30 minutes, or until firm to the touch (it should still be a little soft in the centre). Remove from the oven and leave to cool completely. Sprinkle with the sugar, cut into 20 squares and serve.

double chocolate brownies

makes 9 large or 16 small

115 g/4 oz butter, plus extra
for greasing

115 g/4 oz plain chocolate, broken
into pieces

300 g/10½ oz golden caster sugar

pinch of salt

1 tsp vanilla extract

2 large eggs

140 g/5 oz plain flour

2 tbsp cocoa powder

100 g/3½ oz white
chocolate chips

fudge sauce

55 g/2 oz butter

225 g/8 oz golden caster sugar

150 ml/5 fl oz milk

250 ml/9 fl oz double cream

225 g/8 oz golden syrup

200 g/7 oz plain chocolate,
broken into pieces

Preheat the oven to 180°C/350°F/Gas Mark 4. Grease and line the base of an 18-cm/7-inch square baking tin.

Place the butter and chocolate in a small heatproof bowl set over a saucepan of gently simmering water until melted. Stir until smooth. Leave to cool slightly. Stir in the sugar, salt and vanilla extract. Add the eggs, one at a time, and beat until well blended.

Sift the flour and cocoa powder into the mixture and beat until smooth. Stir in the chocolate chips, then pour the mixture into the tin. Bake in the preheated oven for 35–40 minutes, or until the top is evenly coloured and a skewer inserted into the centre comes out almost clean. Leave to cool slightly while preparing the sauce.

To make the sauce, place the butter, sugar, milk, cream and syrup in a small saucepan and heat gently until the sugar has dissolved. Bring to the boil and stir for 10 minutes, or until the mixture is caramel-coloured. Remove from the heat and add the chocolate. Stir until smooth. Cut the brownies into squares and serve immediately with the sauce.

sticky chocolate brownies

makes 9

85 g/3 oz butter, unsalted for preference, plus extra for greasing

140 g/5 oz caster sugar

100 g/3¹/2 oz soft brown sugar

125 g/4¹/2 oz plain chocolate

1 tbsp golden syrup

2 eggs

1 tsp chocolate extract or vanilla extract

100 g/3¹/2 oz plain flour

2 tbsp cocoa powder, plus extra for dusting

¹/2 tsp baking powder

Preheat the oven to 180°C/350°F/Gas Mark 4. Lightly grease a 20-cm/8-inch square baking tin and line the base.

Place the butter, sugars, chocolate and golden syrup in a heavy-based saucepan and heat gently, stirring until the mixture is well blended and smooth. Remove from the heat and leave to cool.

Beat together the eggs and chocolate extract. Whisk in the cooled chocolate mixture. Sift together the flour, cocoa and baking powder and fold carefully into the egg and chocolate mixture using a metal spoon or palette knife.

Spoon the cake mixture into the prepared tin and bake in the preheated oven for 25 minutes, until the top is crisp and the edge of the cake is starting to shrink away from the tin. The inside of the cake will still be quite gooey and soft to the touch.

Leave the cake to cool completely in the tin, dust with cocoa powder, then cut it into squares and serve.

white chocolate brownies

makes 9

115 g/4 oz butter, plus extra
for greasing
225 g/8 oz white chocolate
75 g/2³/4 oz walnut pieces
2 eggs
115 g/4 oz soft brown sugar
115 g/4 oz self-raising flour

Preheat the oven to 180°C/350°F/Gas Mark 4. Lightly grease an 18-cm/7-inch square baking tin.

Coarsely chop 175 g/6 oz of the chocolate and all the walnuts. Put the remaining chocolate and the butter in a heatproof bowl set over a saucepan of gently simmering water. When melted, stir together, then set aside to cool slightly.

Whisk the eggs and sugar together, then beat in the cooled chocolate mixture until well mixed. Fold in the flour, chopped chocolate and the walnuts. Turn the mixture into the prepared tin and smooth the surface.

Transfer the tin to the preheated oven and bake the brownies for about 30 minutes, until just set. The mixture should still be a little soft in the centre. Leave to cool in the tin, then cut into 9 squares before serving.

chocolate chip brownies

makes 12

225 g/8 oz butter, softened,
plus extra for greasing
150 g/5^1/$_2$ oz plain chocolate,
broken into pieces
280 g/10 oz plain flour
100 g/3^1/$_2$ oz caster sugar
4 eggs, beaten
75 g/2^3/$_4$ oz chopped
pistachio nuts
100 g/3^1/$_2$ oz white chocolate,
chopped coarsely
icing sugar, for dusting (optional)

Preheat the oven to 180°C/350°F/Gas Mark 4. Lightly grease and line a 23-cm/9-inch square baking tin.

Melt the plain chocolate and butter in a heatproof bowl set over a saucepan of gently simmering water. Leave to cool slightly.

Sift the flour into a separate mixing bowl and stir in the caster sugar.

Stir the eggs into the melted chocolate mixture, then pour this mixture into the flour and sugar mixture, beating well. Stir in the pistachio nuts and white chocolate, then pour the mixture into the tin, spreading it evenly into the corners.

Bake in the preheated oven for 30–35 minutes, until firm to the touch. Leave to cool in the tin for 20 minutes, then turn out onto a wire rack.

Leave to cool completely, then cut into 12 pieces and dust with icing sugar, if using.

cappuccino brownies

makes 15

225 g/8 oz butter, softened, plus
extra for greasing

225 g/8 oz self-raising flour

1 tsp baking powder

1 tsp cocoa powder, plus
extra for dusting

225 g/8 oz golden caster sugar

4 eggs, beaten

3 tbsp instant coffee granules,
dissolved in 2 tbsp hot water,
cooled

cocoa powder, for dusting

white chocolate frosting

115 g/4 oz white chocolate,
broken into pieces

55 g/2 oz butter, softened

3 tbsp milk

175 g/6 oz icing sugar

Preheat the oven to 180°C/350°F/Gas Mark 4. Grease and line the base of a shallow 28 x 18-cm/11 x 7-inch rectangular baking tin.

Sift the flour, baking powder and cocoa into a bowl and add the butter, caster sugar, eggs and coffee. Beat well, by hand or with an electric whisk, until smooth, then spoon into the prepared tin and smooth the top.

Bake in the oven for 35–40 minutes, or until risen and firm. Leave to cool in the tin for 10 minutes, then turn out onto a wire rack and peel off the lining paper. Leave to cool completely.

To make the frosting, place the chocolate, butter and milk in a bowl set over a saucepan of simmering water and stir until the chocolate has melted. Remove the bowl from the saucepan and sift in the icing sugar. Beat until smooth, then spread over the cake. Dust the top of the cake with sifted cocoa powder, then cut into squares.

mocha brownies

makes 16

55 g/2 oz butter, plus extra
for greasing
115 g/4 oz plain chocolate,
broken into pieces
175 g/6 oz dark muscovado sugar
2 eggs
1 tbsp instant coffee granules,
dissolved in 1 tbsp hot
water, cooled
85 g/3 oz plain flour
1/2 tsp baking powder
55 g/2 oz pecan nuts,
roughly chopped

decoration
100 g/3 1/2 oz golden icing sugar
1–2 tbsp water
chopped pecan nuts

Preheat the oven to 180°C/350°F/Gas Mark 4. Grease and line the base of a 20-cm/8-inch square baking tin.

Place the chocolate and butter in a heavy-based saucepan over a low heat until melted. Stir and leave to cool.

Place the sugar and eggs in a large bowl and cream together until light and fluffy. Fold in the chocolate mixture and cooled coffee and mix thoroughly. Sift in the flour and baking powder and lightly fold into the mixture. Carefully fold in the pecan nuts.

Pour the mixture into the prepared tin and bake in the preheated oven for 25–30 minutes, or until firm and a skewer inserted into the centre comes out clean.

Leave to cool in the tin for a few minutes, then run a knife around the edge of the cake to loosen it. Turn the cake out onto a wire rack and peel off the lining paper. Leave to cool completely. When cold, cut into squares.

Mix the golden icing sugar with the water to give a pouring consistency. Trickle over or around each brownie and sprinkle with chopped pecan nuts.

ginger chocolate chip brownies

makes 24

4 pieces stem ginger in syrup
225 g/8 oz plain flour
1¹/₂ tsp ground ginger
1 tsp ground cinnamon
¹/₄ tsp ground cloves
¹/₄ tsp grated nutmeg
115 g/4 oz soft brown sugar
115 g/4 oz butter
115 g/4 oz golden syrup
100 g/3¹/₂ oz plain chocolate chips

Preheat the oven to 150°C/300°F/Gas Mark 2.

Finely chop the stem ginger. Sift the flour, ground ginger, cinnamon, cloves and nutmeg into a large bowl. Stir in the chopped stem ginger and sugar.

Put the butter and the syrup into a saucepan and heat gently until melted. Bring to the boil, then pour the mixture into the flour mixture, stirring all the time. Beat until the mixture is cool enough to handle.

Add the chocolate chips to the mixture. Press evenly into a 30 x 20-cm/12 x 8-inch rectangular baking tin.

Transfer to the oven and bake for 30 minutes. Cut into fingers, then leave to cool in the tin.

super mocha brownies

makes 12

100 g/3¹/2 oz butter, plus extra
for greasing
150 g/5¹/2 oz good-quality plain
dark chocolate (about 70 per
cent cocoa solids)
1 tsp strong instant coffee
1 tsp vanilla extract
100 g/3¹/2 oz ground almonds
175 g/6 oz caster sugar
4 eggs, separated
icing sugar, to decorate (optional)

Preheat the oven to 180°C/350°F/Gas Mark 4. Grease a 20-cm/8-inch square baking tin and line the base.

Melt the chocolate and butter in a heatproof bowl placed over a saucepan of gently simmering water, making sure that the bottom of the bowl does not touch the water. Stir very occasionally until the chocolate and butter have melted and are smooth.

Carefully remove the bowl from the heat. Leave to cool slightly, then stir in the coffee and vanilla extract. Add the almonds and sugar and mix well until combined. Lightly beat the egg yolks in a separate bowl, then stir into the chocolate mixture.

Whisk the egg whites in a large bowl until they form stiff peaks. Gently fold a large spoonful of the egg whites into the chocolate mixture, then fold in the remainder until completely incorporated.

Spoon the mixture into the prepared tin and bake in the preheated oven for 35–40 minutes, or until risen and firm on top but still slightly gooey in the centre. Leave to cool in the tin, then turn out, remove the lining paper and cut into 12 pieces. Dust with icing sugar before serving, if using.

naughty but nice

new twists

soured cream brownies

makes 9 large or 16 small

55 g/2 oz butter, plus extra
for greasing

115 g/4 oz plain chocolate,
broken into pieces

175 g/6 oz soft brown sugar

2 eggs

2 tbsp strong coffee, cooled

85 g/3 oz plain flour

1/2 tsp baking powder

pinch of salt

55 g/2 oz walnuts, chopped

mini chocolate balls, to decorate

frosting

115 g/4 oz plain chocolate,
broken into pieces

150 ml/5 fl oz soured cream

Preheat the oven to 180°C/350°F/Gas Mark 4. Grease and line a 20-cm/8-inch square baking tin.

Place the chocolate and butter in a small heatproof bowl set over a saucepan of gently simmering water until melted. Stir until smooth. Remove from the heat and leave to cool.

Beat the sugar and eggs together until pale and thick. Fold in the chocolate mixture and coffee. Mix well. Sift the flour, baking powder and salt into the mixture and fold in. Fold in the walnuts. Pour the mixture into the tin and bake in the oven for 20–25 minutes, or until set. Leave to cool in the tin.

To make the frosting, place the chocolate in a heatproof bowl set over a saucepan of gently simmering water and stir until melted. Stir in the soured cream and beat until evenly blended. Spoon the topping over the brownies and make a swirling pattern with a palette knife. Leave to set in a cool place. Cut into bars, then remove from the tin and serve, decorated with mini chocolate balls.

walnut & cinnamon blondies

makes 9

115 g/4 oz butter, plus extra
for greasing
225 g/8 oz soft brown sugar
1 egg
1 egg yolk
140 g/5 oz self-raising flour
1 tsp ground cinnamon
85 g/3 oz coarsely chopped
walnuts

Preheat the oven to 180°C/350°F/Gas Mark 4. Grease and line the base of an 18-cm/7-inch square baking tin.

Place the butter and sugar in a saucepan over a low heat and stir until the sugar has dissolved. Cook, stirring, for a further 1 minute. The mixture will bubble slightly, but do not let it boil. Leave to cool for 10 minutes.

Stir the egg and egg yolk into the mixture. Sift in the flour and cinnamon, add the nuts and stir until just blended. Pour the cake mixture into the prepared tin, then bake in the preheated oven for 20–25 minutes, or until springy in the centre and a skewer inserted into the centre of the cake comes out clean.

Leave to cool in the tin for a few minutes, then run a knife around the edge of the cake to loosen it. Turn the cake out onto a wire rack and peel off the paper. Leave to cool completely. When cold, cut into squares.

upside-down toffee apple brownies

makes 9

toffee apple topping
85 g/3 oz light muscovado sugar
55 g/2 oz unsalted butter
1 dessert apple, cored and thinly sliced

brownies
115 g/4 oz unsalted butter, plus extra for greasing
175 g/6 oz light muscovado sugar
2 eggs, beaten
200 g/7 oz plain flour
1 tsp baking powder
$1/2$ tsp bicarbonate of soda
$1^1/2$ tsp ground mixed spice
2 eating apples, peeled and coarsely grated
85 g/3 oz hazelnuts, chopped

Preheat the oven to 180°C/350°F/Gas Mark 4. Grease a 23-cm/9-inch square shallow baking tin.

For the topping, place the muscovado sugar and butter in a small pan and heat gently, stirring, until melted. Pour into the prepared tin. Arrange the apple slices over the mixture.

For the brownies, place the butter and sugar in a bowl and beat well until pale and fluffy. Beat in the eggs gradually.

Sift together the flour, baking powder, bicarbonate of soda and mixed spice, and fold into the mixture. Stir in the apples and nuts.

Pour into the prepared tin and bake for 35–40 minutes, until firm and golden. Cool in the tin for 10 minutes, then turn out and cut into squares.

rocky road brownies

makes 16

225 g/8 oz butter, melted,
plus extra for greasing

100 g/3$^{1}/_{2}$ oz plain flour, plus extra
for dusting

140 g/5 oz caster sugar

3 tbsp cocoa

$^{1}/_{2}$ tsp baking powder

2 eggs, beaten

1 tsp vanilla extract

70 g/2$^{1}/_{2}$ oz glacé cherries,
quartered

70 g/2$^{1}/_{2}$ oz blanched almonds,
chopped

100 g/3$^{1}/_{2}$ oz marshmallows,
chopped

fudge frosting

200 g/7 oz icing sugar

2 tbsp cocoa

3 tbsp evaporated milk

$^{1}/_{2}$ tsp vanilla extract

Preheat the oven to 160°C/325°F/Gas Mark 3. Grease a 23-cm/9-inch square shallow baking tin and dust lightly with flour.

Sift together the flour, sugar, cocoa and baking powder and make a well in the centre. Stir in the melted butter, eggs and vanilla extract and beat well to mix thoroughly.

Stir in the cherries and almonds. Pour into the prepared tin and bake for 35–40 minutes, until just firm on top. Leave to cool in the tin.

Meanwhile, make the frosting. Place all the ingredients in a large bowl and beat well to mix to a smooth, just spreadable consistency.

Spread the cooled brownies with the frosting, swirling lightly, and sprinkle with marshmallows. Leave until the frosting sets, then cut into squares.

rich apricot blondies

makes 12

350 g/12 oz white chocolate

85 g/3 oz unsalted butter, plus
extra for greasing

1 tsp vanilla extract

3 eggs, beaten

140 g/5$^{1}/_{2}$ oz light muscovado
sugar

115 g/4 oz self-raising flour

85 g/3 oz macadamia nuts,
roughly chopped

100 g/3$^{1}/_{2}$ oz ready-to-eat dried
apricots, roughly chopped

Preheat the oven to 190°C/375°F/Gas Mark 5. Lightly grease a 28 x 18-cm/11 x 7-inch rectangular baking tin and line the base.

Chop half the chocolate into small chunks. Melt the remaining chocolate with the butter in a small pan over a very low heat and stir until melted. Remove from the heat and stir in the vanilla extract.

Whisk the eggs and sugar together in a large bowl until pale. Beat in the melted chocolate mixture. Fold in the flour evenly, then stir in the macadamia nuts, apricots and chopped chocolate.

Spoon into the tin and smooth the top level. Bake for 25–30 minutes, or until firm and golden brown.

Leave to cool in the tin. Turn out when cold and cut into triangles or squares.

pecan brownie muffins

makes 12

115 g/4 oz pecan nuts
100 g/3$\frac{1}{2}$ oz plain flour
175 g/6 oz caster sugar
$\frac{1}{4}$ tsp salt
1 tbsp baking powder
225 g/8 oz unsalted butter
115 g/4 oz plain chocolate
4 eggs, beaten
1 tsp vanilla extract

Preheat the oven to 200°C/400°F/Gas Mark 6. Place paper muffin cases in a 12-cup muffin tin. Reserve 12 pecan halves and roughly chop the rest.

Sift the flour, sugar, salt and baking powder into a large bowl and make a well in the centre. Melt the butter and chocolate in a small pan over a very low heat, stirring frequently. Add to the flour mixture and stir to mix evenly.

Add the eggs and vanilla extract and mix together just until the ingredients are evenly moistened. Stir in the chopped pecans.

Spoon the batter into the muffin cases, filling each about three-quarters full. Add a pecan half on top of each. Bake for 20–25 minutes, or until well risen and firm to the touch.

marbled choc cheesecake brownies

makes 12

175 g/6 oz unsalted butter, plus extra for greasing

3 tbsp cocoa

200 g/7 oz golden caster sugar

2 eggs, beaten

125 g/4^{1}/2 oz plain flour

cheesecake mix

250 g/9 oz ricotta cheese

40 g/1^{1}/2 oz golden caster sugar

1 egg, beaten

Preheat the oven to 180°C/350°F/Gas Mark 4. Grease a 28 x 18-cm/11 x 7-inch rectangular baking tin.

Melt the butter in a medium saucepan, remove from the heat and stir in the cocoa and sugar. Beat in the eggs, then add the flour and stir to mix evenly. Pour into the prepared tin.

For the cheesecake mix, beat together the ricotta, sugar and egg, then drop teaspoonfuls of the mixture over the chocolate mixture. Use a palette knife to swirl the two mixtures together lightly.

Bake in the preheated oven for 40–45 minutes, until just firm to the touch. Cool in the tin, then cut into bars or squares.

maple-glazed pistachio brownies

makes 16

175 g/6 oz unsalted butter, plus
extra for greasing
115 g/4 oz plain chocolate
250 g/9 oz caster sugar
4 eggs, beaten
1 tsp vanilla extract
200 g/7 oz plain flour
85 g/3 oz pistachio nuts, skinned
and chopped

glaze

115 g/4 oz plain chocolate
115 g/4 oz crème fraîche
2 tbsp maple syrup

Preheat the oven to 190°C/375°F/Gas Mark 5. Lightly grease a 30 x 20-cm/12 x 8-inch rectangular shallow baking tin.

Place the chocolate with the butter in a small pan over a very low heat and stir until melted. Remove from the heat.

Whisk the sugar, eggs and vanilla extract together in a large bowl until pale. Beat in the melted chocolate mixture. Fold in the flour evenly, then stir in 55 g/2 oz of the pistachio nuts.

Spoon into the tin and smooth the top level. Bake for 25–30 minutes, or until firm and golden brown.

For the glaze, melt the chocolate in a heatproof bowl set over a pan of gently simmering water. Stir in the crème fraîche and maple syrup and beat until smooth and glossy.

Spread the glaze over the brownies evenly with a palette knife. Sprinkle with the remaining pistachio nuts and leave until the topping is set. Cut into squares.

cranberry soured cream brownies

makes 12

115 g/4 oz unsalted butter, plus
extra for greasing
4 tbsp cocoa powder
200 g/7 oz light muscovado sugar
140 g/5 oz self-raising flour, plus
extra for dusting
2 eggs, beaten
115 g/4 oz fresh cranberries

topping

150 ml/5 fl oz soured cream
1 tbsp caster sugar
1 tbsp self-raising flour
1 egg yolk
1/2 tsp vanilla extract

Preheat the oven to 180°C/350°F/Gas 4. Grease a 30 x 20-cm/12 x 8-inch rectangular

shallow baking tin and dust lightly with flour.

Place the butter, cocoa and sugar in a pan and stir over a low heat until just melted.

Remove from the heat and cool slightly.

Quickly stir in the flour and eggs and beat hard until thoroughly mixed to a smooth batter.

Stir in the cranberries, then spread the mixture into the prepared tin.

For the topping, beat together all the ingredients until smooth, then spoon over the

chocolate mixture, swirling evenly with a palette knife.

Bake for 35–40 minutes, or until risen and firm. Cool in the tin, then cut into squares.

low-fat banana cardamom brownies

makes 16

butter, for greasing
115 g/4 oz plain flour
3 tbsp cocoa powder
2 tbsp dried milk powder
1/4 tsp baking powder
1/4 tsp salt
2 ripe bananas
150 g/5 1/2 oz light muscovado
sugar
2 egg whites
150 g/5 1/2 oz low-fat natural yogurt
seeds from 2 cardamom pods,
crushed
shredded coconut, toasted,
to decorate

Preheat the oven to 180°C/350°F/Gas Mark 4. Grease a 23-cm/9-inch square shallow baking tin.

Sift the flour, cocoa, milk powder, baking powder and salt into a large bowl and make a well in the centre.

Mash the bananas and beat with the sugar, egg whites, yogurt and cardamom seeds. Stir into the dry ingredients, mixing evenly.

Spoon into the prepared tin and bake for 25–30 minutes, or until just firm. Cool in the tin, then cut into squares. Decorate with shredded coconut.

carrot streusel brownies

makes 15

115 g/4 oz unsalted butter,
softened, plus extra for greasing

350 g/10^1/2 oz light muscovado
sugar

2 eggs, beaten

1 tsp vanilla extract

175 g/6 oz plain flour

^{1}/2 tsp bicarbonate of soda

^{1}/2 tsp baking powder

85 g/3 oz sultanas

125 g/4^1/2 oz carrots, finely grated

55 g/2 oz walnuts, chopped

streusel topping

40 g/1^1/2 oz finely chopped
walnuts

40 g/1^1/2 oz dark muscovado
sugar

15 g/^{1}/2 oz plain flour

^{1}/2 tsp ground cinnamon

15 g/^{1}/2 oz unsalted butter, melted

Preheat the oven to 180°C/350°F/Gas Mark 4. Grease a 30 x 20-cm/12 x 8-inch rectangular shallow baking tin.

Cream together the sugar and butter until pale. Beat in the eggs and vanilla extract. Sift the flour, bicarbonate of soda and baking powder into the mixture and fold in evenly. Stir in the sultanas, carrots and walnuts.

Spread the mixture into the prepared tin. Mix together all the topping ingredients to make a crumbly mixture and sprinkle evenly over the cake mixture.

Bake in the oven for 45–55 minutes, or until golden brown and just firm to the touch.

Cool in the tin, then cut into bars or squares.

pure luxury

made to impress

mint julep brownie cakes

makes 6–8

175 g/6 oz unsalted butter, plus extra for greasing

125 g/4½ oz self-raising flour, plus extra for dusting

150 g/5½ oz plain chocolate

2 eggs

200 g/7 oz dark muscovado sugar

3 tbsp bourbon

1 tbsp chopped fresh mint

mint sprigs, to decorate

sauce

115 g/4 oz plain chocolate

125 ml/4 fl oz single cream

¼ tsp peppermint extract

Preheat the oven to 180°C/350°F/Gas Mark 4. Grease and flour a 28 x 18-cm/ 11 x 7-inch rectangular baking tin.

Place the chocolate and butter in a pan over a very low heat and stir occasionally until melted. Remove from the heat.

Beat together the eggs, sugar, bourbon and chopped mint, then beat quickly into the chocolate mixture. Fold in the flour and mix evenly.

Pour the mixture into the prepared tin and smooth the surface. Bake in the oven for 30–35 minutes, until just firm, but still slightly soft inside.

Allow to cool in the tin for 15 minutes, then remove from the tin and use a 7.5-cm/3-inch cutter to stamp out 6–8 rounds.

For the sauce, place the chocolate, cream and peppermint extract in a small pan and heat gently, stirring, until melted and smooth.

To serve, place the brownie cakes on serving plates, drizzle with the chocolate sauce and decorate with sprigs of mint.

brownie base cheesecake

makes 12

brownie base

115 g/4 oz unsalted butter,
plus extra for greasing

115 g/4 oz plain chocolate

200 g/7 oz caster sugar

2 eggs, beaten

50 ml /2 fl oz milk

115 g/4 oz plain flour, plus extra
for dusting

strawberries dipped in melted plain
chocolate, to decorate

topping

500 g/1 lb 2 oz soft cheese

125 g/4½ oz golden caster sugar

3 eggs, beaten

1 tsp vanilla extract

115 g/4 oz natural yogurt

melted plain chocolate, to drizzle

Preheat the oven to 180°C/350°F/Gas Mark 4. Lightly grease and flour a 23-cm/9-inch square baking tin.

Melt the butter and chocolate in a saucepan over a low heat, stirring until smooth. Remove from the heat and beat in the sugar.

Add the eggs and milk, beating well. Stir in the flour, mixing just until blended. Spoon into the prepared tin, spreading evenly.

Bake in the oven for 25 minutes. Remove from the oven and reduce the oven temperature to 160°C/325°F/Gas Mark 3.

For the topping, beat together the cheese, sugar, eggs and vanilla extract until well blended. Stir in the yogurt, then pour over the brownie base. Bake for a further 45–55 minutes, or until the centre is almost set.

Run a knife around the edge of the cake to loosen from the tin. Let cool before removing from the tin. Chill in the refrigerator for 4 hours or overnight before cutting into slices. Serve drizzled with melted chocolate and with the chocolate-dipped strawberries on the side.

black Russian brownies

makes 8–10

115 g/4 oz unsalted butter, plus extra for greasing

115 g/4 oz plain chocolate

1/2 tsp coarsely ground black peppercorns

4 eggs, beaten

250 g/9 oz caster sugar

1/2 tsp vanilla extract

3 tbsp Kahlúa liqueur

2 tbsp vodka

150 g/5 1/2 oz plain flour

1/4 tsp baking powder

55 g/2 oz chopped walnuts, plus extra to decorate

cocoa powder, to decorate

Kahlúa cream topping

2 tbsp Kahlúa liqueur

200 g/7 oz crème fraîche

Preheat the oven to 180°C/350°F/Gas Mark 4. Grease and line the base of a 30 x 20-cm/12 x 8-inch rectangular shallow baking tin.

Melt the chocolate and the butter with the peppercorns in a small saucepan over a low heat. Remove from the heat and cool slightly.

Beat together the eggs, sugar and vanilla extract in a large bowl and stir in the chocolate mixture, Kahlúa and vodka.

Sift the flour and baking powder and stir evenly into the chocolate mixture. Stir in the walnuts. Pour into the tin and bake in the oven for 20–25 minutes, until just firm to the touch.

Cool for a few minutes, then cut into bars or squares and lift carefully from the tin onto serving plates.

For the topping, stir the Kahlúa into the crème fraîche and spoon a generous dollop on each serving of brownie. Sprinkle with a little cocoa, decorate with walnuts and serve immediately.

mochachino brownies with white mocha sauce

makes 8–9

115 g/4 oz unsalted butter, plus
extra for greasing

115 g/4 oz plain chocolate

2 tbsp strong black coffee

250 g/9 oz golden caster sugar

1/2 tsp ground cinnamon

3 eggs, beaten

85 g/3 oz plain flour

55 g/2 oz milk chocolate chips

55 g/2 oz toasted walnuts,
skinned and chopped, plus extra
to decorate

white mocha sauce

100 ml/3¹/2 fl oz double cream

85 g/3 oz white chocolate

1 tbsp strong black coffee

Preheat the oven to 180°C/350°F/Gas Mark 4. Grease and line a 23-cm/9-inch square baking tin.

Place the butter, chocolate and coffee in a medium saucepan over a low heat and stir until just melted and smooth. Cool slightly.

Whisk in the sugar, cinnamon and eggs. Beat in the flour, chocolate chips and walnuts. Pour into the prepared tin.

Bake in the oven for 30–35 minutes, until just firm but still moist inside. Cool in the tin then cut into squares or bars.

Meanwhile, make the sauce by placing all the ingredients in a small pan over a low heat, stirring occasionally, until melted and smooth.

Place the brownies on individual plates and spoon the warm sauce on top. Decorate with chopped walnuts and serve.

blonde brownie hearts with raspberry sauce

makes 8

115 g/4 oz unsalted butter, plus
extra for greasing
115 g/4 oz white chocolate
2 eggs, beaten
150 g/5 1/2 oz caster sugar
seeds from 1 vanilla pod
140 g/5 oz plain flour, plus extra
for dusting
8 small squares plain chocolate

raspberry sauce
250 g/9 oz raspberries, fresh or
frozen, thawed
2 tbsp amaretto
1 tbsp icing sugar

Preheat the oven to 180°C/350°F/Gas Mark 4. Grease and lightly flour 8 individual heart-shaped baking tins, each 150 ml/5 fl oz capacity.

Place the chocolate and butter in a pan over a low heat and heat gently, stirring, until just melted. Remove from the heat.

Whisk together the eggs, sugar and vanilla seeds until smooth and thick. Fold in the flour lightly, then stir in the chocolate mixture and mix evenly.

Pour the batter mixture into the tins, adding a square of chocolate to the centre of each, without pressing down. Bake for about 20–25 minutes, until just firm. Leave in the tins for 5 minutes.

To make the raspberry sauce, place half the raspberries, the amaretto and icing sugar in a food processor or blender and process until smooth. Transfer the mixture to a sieve placed on top of a bowl and rub through to remove the pips.

Run a knife around the edge of each heart to loosen from the tin and turn out onto individual plates. Spoon the raspberry sauce around, decorate with the remaining raspberries and serve warm.

Black Forest brownies

makes 8

115 g/4 oz unsalted butter, plus
extra for greasing

85 g/3 oz plain flour

1/2 tsp baking powder

55 g/2 oz cocoa powder

2 eggs, beaten

175 g/6 oz caster sugar

1 tsp vanilla extract

1/2 tsp almond extract

140 g/5 oz pitted dark cherries,
quartered

chocolate curls and whole fresh
cherries, to decorate

cherry cream

150 ml/5 fl oz double cream

1 tbsp kirsch liqueur

Preheat the oven to 180°C/350°F/Gas Mark 4. Grease a 28 x 18-cm/11 x 7-inch rectangular shallow baking tin.

Sift together the flour and baking powder.

Place the butter in a large saucepan over a medium heat and stir until melted. Remove from the heat and add the cocoa, stirring until smooth. Beat in the eggs, sugar, vanilla extract and almond extract.

Fold in the flour mixture and cherries. Pour into the prepared tin and bake for 25–30 minutes, or until just firm to the touch. Cool slightly in the tin.

Cut into squares and remove from the tin. Whip the cream with the kirsch and spoon a little onto each brownie. Decorate with chocolate curls and serve with fresh cherries.

rich ginger brownies with port cream

makes 8

175 g/6 oz unsalted butter, plus
extra for greasing
200 g/7 oz plain chocolate
200 g/7 oz granulated sugar
4 eggs, beaten
2 tsp vanilla extract
1 tbsp stem ginger syrup
100 g/3½ oz plain flour
55 g/2 oz preserved stem ginger
in syrup, chopped
25 g/1 oz chopped crystallised
ginger, to decorate

port cream

200 ml/7 fl oz ruby port
200 ml/7 fl oz double cream
1 tbsp icing sugar
1 tsp vanilla extract

Preheat the oven to 180°C/350°F/Gas Mark 4. Grease a 23-cm/9-inch square shallow baking tin.

Place the chocolate and butter in a saucepan and heat gently, stirring, until melted. Remove from the heat and stir in the sugar.

Beat the eggs, vanilla extract and ginger syrup into the chocolate mixture. Stir in the flour and ginger, mixing evenly.

Pour the mixture into the prepared tin and bake in the oven for 30–35 minutes, until just firm to the touch.

Meanwhile, make the port cream. Place the port in a saucepan and simmer over a medium-high heat until reduced to about 4 tablespoons. Cool. Whip the cream until beginning to thicken, then beat in the sugar, reduced port and vanilla extract, continuing to whip until it holds soft peaks.

Remove the brownies from the oven, cool for 2–3 minutes in the tin, then cut into 8 triangles. Place on individual serving plates and add a spoonful of port cream to each. Top with pieces of crystallised ginger and serve warm.

heavenly bites

traybake treats

chocolate peanut butter squares

makes 20

300 g/10^{1}/$_{2}$ oz milk chocolate
350 g/12 oz plain flour
1 tsp baking powder
225 g/8 oz butter
350 g/12 oz soft brown sugar
175 g/6 oz rolled oats
70 g/2^{1}/$_{2}$ oz chopped mixed nuts
1 egg, beaten
400 g/14 oz condensed milk
70 g/2^{1}/$_{2}$ oz crunchy peanut butter

Preheat the oven to 180°C/350°F/Gas Mark 4.

Finely chop the chocolate. Sift the flour and baking powder into a large bowl.

Add the butter to the flour and rub in until the mixture resembles breadcrumbs. Stir in the sugar, oats and chopped nuts.

Put a quarter of the mixture into a bowl and stir in the chopped chocolate. Set aside.

Stir the egg into the remaining mixture, then press into the bottom of a 30 x 20-cm/ 12 x 8-inch rectangular baking tin.

Bake the base in the preheated oven for 15 minutes. Meanwhile, mix the condensed milk and peanut butter together. Pour the mixture over the base and spread evenly, then sprinkle the reserved chocolate mixture on top and press down lightly.

Return to the oven and bake for a further 20 minutes, until golden brown. Leave to cool in the tin, then cut into squares.

almond slices

makes 8

3 eggs
60 g/2¼ oz ground almonds
140 g/5 oz dried milk powder
200 g/7 oz granulated sugar
½ tsp saffron threads
115 g/4 oz unsalted butter
1 tbsp flaked almonds

Preheat the oven to 160°C/325°F/Gas Mark 3.

Lightly beat the eggs together in a mixing bowl and set aside.

Place the ground almonds, milk powder, sugar and saffron in a large mixing bowl and stir to mix well.

Melt the butter in a small saucepan over a low heat. Pour the melted butter over the dry ingredients and mix well with a wooden spoon until thoroughly combined. Add the beaten eggs to the mixture and stir to blend well.

Spread the mixture evenly in a shallow 20-cm/8-inch square baking tin, sprinkle with the almonds and bake in the preheated oven for 45 minutes, or until a skewer inserted into the centre comes out clean.

Remove from the oven and cut into triangles or slices. Transfer to serving plates and serve hot or cold.

chocolate marshmallow fingers

makes 18

350 g/12 oz digestive biscuits

125 g/4¹/2 oz plain chocolate, broken into pieces

225 g/8 oz butter

25 g/1 oz caster sugar

2 tbsp cocoa powder

2 tbsp honey

55 g/2 oz mini marshmallows

100 g/3¹/2 oz white chocolate chips

Put the digestive biscuits in a polythene bag and, using a rolling pin, crush into small pieces.

Put the chocolate, butter, sugar, cocoa and honey in a saucepan and heat gently until melted. Remove from the heat and leave to cool slightly.

Stir the crushed biscuits into the chocolate mixture until well mixed. Add the marshmallows and mix well, then finally stir in the chocolate chips.

Turn the mixture into a 20-cm/8-inch square baking tin and lightly smooth the top. Put in the refrigerator and leave to chill for 2–3 hours, until set. Cut into fingers before serving.

macadamia nut caramel squares

makes 16

base
115 g/4 oz macadamia nuts
280 g/10 oz plain flour
175 g/6 oz soft brown sugar
115 g/4 oz butter

topping
115 g/4 oz butter
100 g/3¹/2 oz soft brown sugar
200 g/7 oz milk chocolate chips

Preheat the oven to 180°C/350°F/Gas Mark 4.

Coarsely chop the macadamia nuts. To make the base, beat together the flour, sugar and butter until the mixture resembles fine breadcrumbs.

Press the mixture into the bottom of a 30 x 20-cm/12 x 8-inch rectangular baking tin. Sprinkle over the macadamia nuts.

To make the topping, put the butter and sugar in a saucepan and, stirring constantly, slowly bring the mixture to the boil. Boil for 1 minute, stirring constantly, then carefully pour the mixture over the macadamia nuts.

Bake in the preheated oven for about 20 minutes, until the caramel topping is bubbling. Remove from the oven and immediately sprinkle the chocolate chips evenly on top. Leave for 2–3 minutes, until the chocolate chips start to melt then, using the blade of a knife, swirl the chocolate over the top. Leave to cool in the tin, then cut into squares.

hazelnut chocolate crunch

makes 12

115 g/4 oz unsalted butter, plus
extra for greasing
200 g/7 oz rolled oats
55 g/2 oz hazelnuts, lightly toasted
and chopped
55 g/2 oz plain flour
85 g/3 oz light muscovado sugar
2 tbsp golden syrup
55 g/2 oz plain chocolate chips

Preheat the oven to 180°C/350°F/Gas Mark 4. Grease a 23-cm/9-inch square shallow baking tin.

Mix the oats, hazelnuts and flour in a large bowl.

Place the butter, sugar and syrup in a large saucepan and heat gently until the sugar has dissolved. Pour in the dry ingredients and mix well. Stir in the chocolate chips.

Turn the mixture into the prepared tin and bake in the preheated oven for 20–25 minutes, or until golden brown and firm to the touch. Using a knife, mark into 12 triangles and leave to cool in the tin. Cut the hazelnut chocolate crunch triangles with a sharp knife before carefully removing them from the tin.

fruity flapjacks

makes 14

sunflower oil, for brushing
140 g/5 oz rolled oats
115 g/4 oz demerara sugar
85 g/3 oz raisins
115 g/4 oz butter, melted

Preheat the oven to 190°C/375°F/Gas Mark 5. Lightly brush a 28 x 18-cm/11 x 7-inch rectangular shallow baking tin with oil.

Combine the oats, sugar and raisins with the butter, stirring well.

Spoon the oat mixture into the tin and press down firmly with the back of a spoon. Bake in the preheated oven for 15–20 minutes, or until golden.

Using a sharp knife, score lines to mark out 14 bars, then leave to cool in the tin for 10 minutes. Carefully transfer the bars to a wire rack to cool completely.

caramel chocolate shortbread

makes 12

shortbread

115 g/4 oz unsalted butter, plus extra for greasing

175 g/6 oz plain flour

55 g/2 oz golden caster sugar

filling and topping

200 g/7 oz butter

115 g/4 oz golden caster sugar

3 tbsp golden syrup

400 ml/14 fl oz canned condensed milk

200 g/7 oz plain chocolate, broken into pieces

Preheat the oven to 180°C/350°F/Gas Mark 4. Grease and line the base of a 23-cm/9-inch square shallow baking tin.

Place the butter, flour and sugar in a food processor and process until they begin to bind together. Press the mixture into the prepared tin and smooth the top. Bake in the preheated oven for 20–25 minutes, or until golden.

Meanwhile, make the filling. Place the butter, sugar, syrup and condensed milk in a saucepan and heat gently until the sugar has dissolved. Bring to the boil and simmer for 6–8 minutes, stirring constantly, until the mixture becomes very thick. Remove the shortbread base from the oven, pour over the filling and chill in the refrigerator until firm.

To make the topping, melt the chocolate in a heatproof bowl set over a saucepan of gently simmering water. Remove from the heat, leave to cool slightly, then spread over the caramel. Chill in the refrigerator until set. Cut it into 12 pieces with a sharp knife and serve.

cinnamon squares

makes 16

225 g/8 oz butter, softened,
plus extra for greasing

225 g/8 oz caster sugar

3 eggs, lightly beaten

225 g/8 oz self-raising flour

1/2 tsp bicarbonate of soda

1 tbsp ground cinnamon

150 ml/5 fl oz soured cream

55 g/2 oz sunflower seeds

Preheat the oven to 180°C/350°F/Gas Mark 4. Grease a 23-cm/9-inch square baking tin and line the base.

In a large mixing bowl, cream together the butter and caster sugar until the mixture is light and fluffy.

Gradually add the beaten eggs to the mixture, beating thoroughly after each addition.

Sift the flour, bicarbonate of soda and cinnamon together into the creamed mixture and fold in, using a metal spoon in a figure-of-eight movement.

Spoon in the soured cream and sunflower seeds and mix gently until well combined.

Spoon the mixture into the prepared tin and smooth the surface with the back of a spoon or a knife.

Bake in the preheated oven for about 45 minutes, until the mixture is firm to the touch when pressed with a finger.

Loosen the edges with a round-bladed knife, then turn out onto a wire rack to cool completely. Slice into 12 squares before serving.

chocolate peppermint slices

makes 16

55 g/2 oz unsalted butter, plus
extra for greasing
55 g/2 oz caster sugar
115 g/4 oz plain flour
175 g/6 oz icing sugar
1–2 tbsp warm water
1/2 tsp peppermint extract
2 tsp green food colouring
(optional)
175 g/6 oz plain chocolate, broken
into pieces

Preheat the oven to 180°C/350°F/Gas Mark 4. Grease and line a 30 x 20-cm/12 x 8-inch rectangular baking tin.

Beat the butter and sugar together until pale and fluffy. Stir in the flour until the mixture binds together.

Knead the mixture to form a smooth dough, then press into the prepared tin. Prick the surface all over with a fork. Bake in the preheated oven for 10–15 minutes, until lightly browned and just firm to the touch. Remove from the oven and leave to cool in the tin.

Sift the icing sugar into a bowl. Gradually add the water, then add the peppermint extract and food colouring, if using. Spread the icing over the base, then leave to set.

Melt the chocolate in a heatproof bowl set over a saucepan of gently simmering water, remove from the heat, then spread over the icing. Leave to set, then cut into slices.

nutty granola squares

makes 16

115 g/4 oz unsalted butter, plus
extra for greasing
4 tbsp clear honey
25 g/1 oz golden caster sugar
250 g/9 oz rolled oats
25 g/1 oz dried cranberries
25 g/1 oz stoned dates, chopped
25 g/1 oz hazelnuts, chopped
70 g/2¹/₂ oz flaked almonds

Preheat the oven to 375°F/190°C/Gas Mark 5. Grease a 20-cm/8-inch square baking tin.

Melt the butter with the honey and sugar in a pan and stir together. Add the remaining ingredients and mix thoroughly.

Turn the mixture into the prepared tin and press down well. Bake in the preheated oven for 20–30 minutes.

Remove from the oven and let cool in the pan. Cut into 16 squares.

strawberry & chocolate slices

makes 16

225 g/8 oz plain flour
1 tsp baking powder
100 g/3½ oz caster sugar
85 g/3 oz soft brown sugar
225 g/8 oz unsalted butter
150 g/5½ oz rolled oats
225 g/8 oz strawberry jam
100 g/3½ oz plain chocolate chips
25 g/1 oz flaked almonds

Preheat the oven to 190°C/375°F/Gas Mark 5. Line a 30 x 20-cm/12 x 8-inch rectangular deep-sided baking tin.

Sift the flour and baking powder into a large bowl.

Add the caster sugar and brown sugar to the flour and mix well. Add the butter and rub in until the mixture resembles breadcrumbs. Stir in the oats.

Press three-quarters of the mixture into the base of the prepared tin. Bake in the preheated oven for 10 minutes.

Spread the jam over the cooked base, then sprinkle over the chocolate chips. Mix the remaining flour mixture with the almonds. Sprinkle evenly over the chocolate chips and press down gently.

Return to the oven and bake for a further 20–25 minutes, until golden brown. Remove from the oven, leave to cool in the tin, then cut into slices.

apricot flapjacks

makes 10

sunflower oil, for oiling
175 g/6 oz polyunsaturated
margarine
85 g/3 oz demerara sugar
55 g/2 oz clear honey
140 g/5 oz dried apricots,
chopped
2 tsp sesame seeds
225 g/8 oz rolled oats

Preheat the oven to 180°C/350°F/Gas Mark 4. Very lightly oil a 26 x 17-cm/10$^{1/2}$ x 6$^{1/2}$-inch rectangular shallow baking tin.

Put the spread, sugar and honey into a small saucepan over a low heat and heat until the ingredients have melted together – do not boil. When the ingredients are warm and well combined, stir in the apricots, sesame seeds and oats.

Spoon the mixture into the prepared tin and lightly level with the back of a spoon. Cook in the preheated oven for 20–25 minutes, or until golden brown. Remove from the oven, cut into 10 bars and leave to cool completely before removing from the baking tin. Store the flapjacks in an airtight container and consume within 2–3 days.

Index